Mummies

Dana Meachen Rau

mc **Marshall Cavendish**
Benchmark
New York

For Fuzzy, a comforting friend who will last thousands of years
—D.M.R.

Editor: Christina Gardeski
Publisher: Michelle Bisson
Art Director: Anahid Hamparian
Series Designer: Virginia Pope

Printed in Malaysia (T)
135642

Library of Congress Cataloging-in-Publication Data
Rau, Dana Meachen, 1971–
Mummies / by Dana Meachen Rau.
p. cm. — (Bookworms. Surprising science)
Summary: "Discusses the basic scientific principles and historical context of mummies"
—Provided by publisher.
ISBN 978-0-7614-4869-3
1. Mummies—Juvenile literature. I. Title.
GN293.R38 2011
393'.3--dc22
2009053761

Photo research by Connie Gardner

Cover photo by British Museum/Art Resource

The photographs in this book are used by permission and through the courtesy of: *PhotoEdit*: pp. 1, 21 Mark Richards. *The Granger Collection*: pp. 4(L), 8(L), 12, 16(L). *Corbis*: p. 4(R) Gustavo Tomsich; p. 6 Pilar Olivares; p. 9 Ron Watts; p. 11(L) Christophe Boisvieux; p. 16 Charles and Josette Lenars; p. 20 Frans Lanting. *Getty Images*: p. 5 National Geographic; p. 8(R) Hulton Archive; p. 10 Time and Life Pictures, p. 11(R) Stephen L. Alvarez; p. 15 Glen Allison. *The Image Works*: pp. 14(T), 17 akg Images. *Art Resource*: p. 14(B) British Museum; p. 19 Werner Forman. *SuperStock*: p. 18 Prisma. *AP Photo*: p. 3 Amr Nabil.

Mummies

CHAPTER 1

Scientists uncovered these bones and stone tools in a cave in Italy.

Mysterious Remains

Have you ever gone exploring in your backyard or in a park? You might discover some interesting things on the ground. You might find a button or a piece of string. You might spot a candy wrapper or a penny. These small items tell you someone has been there before you. You wonder more about them from these clues.

Bronze pots and pitchers from ancient Rome have lasted thousands of years.

People who lived in this area of Lima, Peru, didn't know that mummies were buried in the soil below them.

Do you wish you could talk to people from long ago? Some scientists spend their lives learning from the dead. They dig up **remains** from the past. Remains might be coins or jewels. They might be buildings, spears, and seeds. Scientists uncover pots, tools, weapons, and even toys. They learn about people from the past by looking at what they left behind.

Scientists sometimes find human remains. A **mummy** is a human body that is hundreds or thousands of years old. It may still have skin, hair, and even clothing. Mummies may seem scary. But they are not scary to scientists. These human remains can tell them a lot about life long ago.

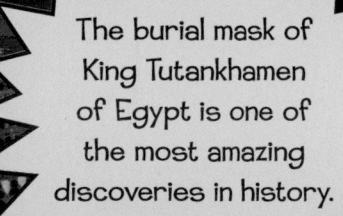

CHAPTER 2

The burial mask of King Tutankhamen of Egypt is one of the most amazing discoveries in history.

Mummy Discoveries

Since the beginning of history, people have lived together in groups. They built villages and cities. These groups grew, changed, or ended. Sometimes land and water covered areas where people once lived. New villages and cities were built on top of the **ruins** of old ones.

Scientists look for traces of these people from the past. This science is called **archaeology**. Archaeologists hike through mountains and deserts. They search forests, caves, and oceans. They set up **digs** to reach remains hidden underground. They have found mummies in Egypt,

At an archaeological dig, scientists carefully remove layers of soil. They take many notes on what they find.

South America, Northern Europe, and all over the world.

In the early 1900s, Howard Carter searched the desert in Egypt. He knew that thousands of years before, Egyptians buried their kings in **tombs**. Many of the tombs he found were empty. Thieves had stolen what was inside. Then in 1922 he found the tomb of King Tutankhamen [too-tahn-KAH-muhn]. The tomb was filled with many treasures, including King Tut's mummy. It wore a beautiful mask of gold.

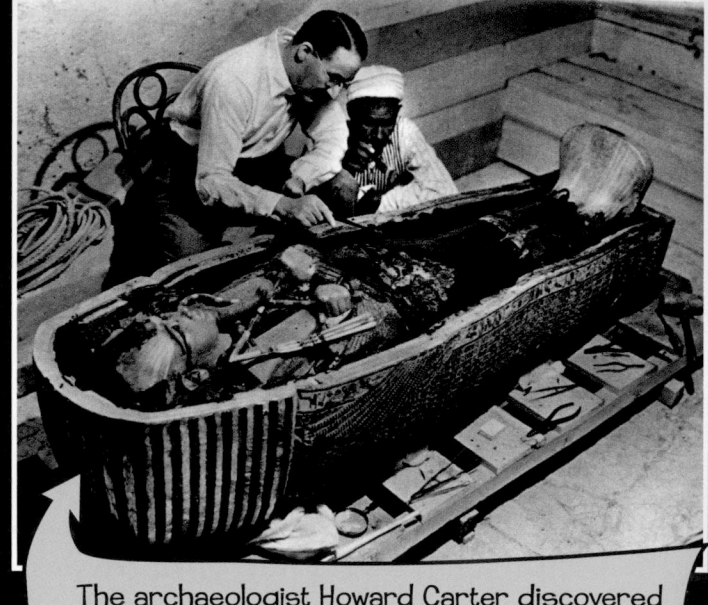

The archaeologist Howard Carter discovered King Tutankhamen's mummy, as well as many other treasures, inside a tomb in 1922.

Some mummies are discovered by accident. In 1950, men were digging in Denmark for a type of soil called **peat**. They needed peat to burn in their fireplaces. They uncovered a man. His skin was stiff and dark, like leather. When scientists looked at the body, they decided it was more than two thousand years old.

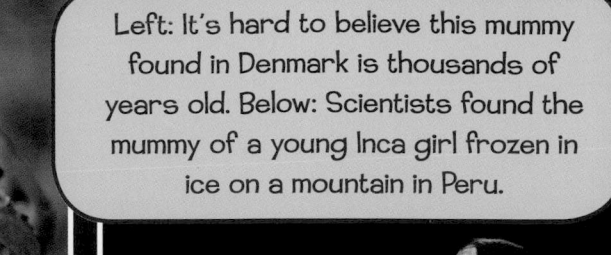

Left: It's hard to believe this mummy found in Denmark is thousands of years old. Below: Scientists found the mummy of a young Inca girl frozen in ice on a mountain in Peru.

In 1995, scientists were hiking in the cold mountains of Peru. They found remains of the Inca people. The Incas lived almost a thousand years ago. One of the scientists noticed a bundle in the ice. It was the mummy of a young Inca girl that they called the Inca Ice Maiden. They carried her down the mountain to study her more closely.

Archaeologists ask questions when they find mummies like these. Who was this person? Why were they buried or left here? What can we find out about the past by looking at these bodies?

CHAPTER 3

The care Egyptians took to make mummies kept the bodies from decaying.

How Mummies Are Made

Not everything can last forever. Some items **decay**. Decay happens when tiny living creatures called **bacteria** break down items and turn them into soil. Natural things, such as cloth, skin, and hair, usually decay quickly. Harder items, such as stone and metal, last much longer.

Mummies are human remains that have not decayed. They may still have skin and hair. They may even be wearing the clothing they had on when they died. How can this be?

Some things do not decay if they are very dry. Think about a raisin. A raisin is really just a dried grape. In the deserts of Egypt, the land is very hot and dry. Long ago, people buried their dead in the sand. The dry sand turned the bodies into mummies. Then the Egyptians started making mummies on purpose. First, they took out the **organs** from the body, such as the stomach, brain, liver, and kidneys. They often left the heart inside. Then they filled and covered the body with a special

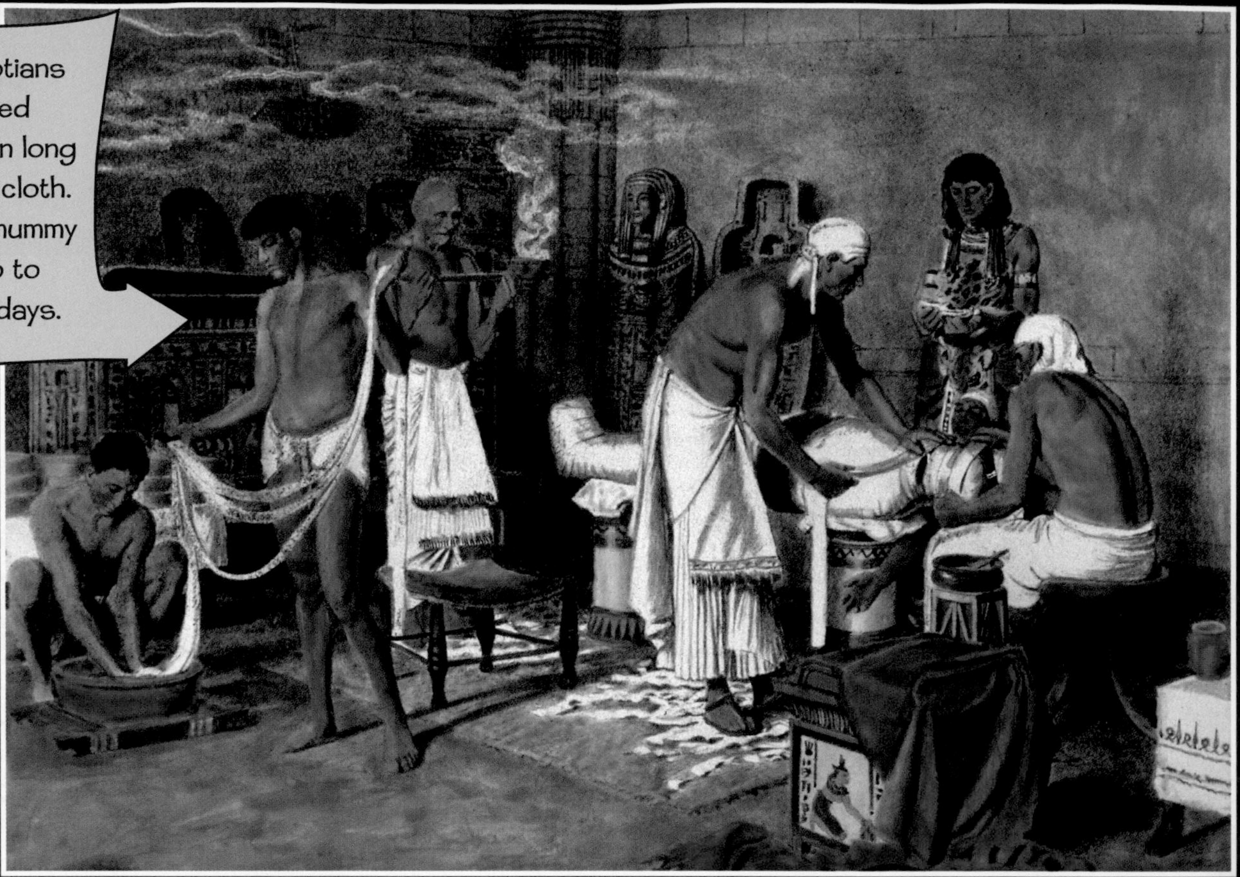

The Egyptians wrapped mummies in long strips of cloth. Making a mummy took up to seventy days.

salt to dry it out. When the body was dry, they stuffed it with sawdust, leaves, or cloth, and covered it with perfume. Then they wrapped the body with long strips of cloth. It took up to seventy days to make a mummy.

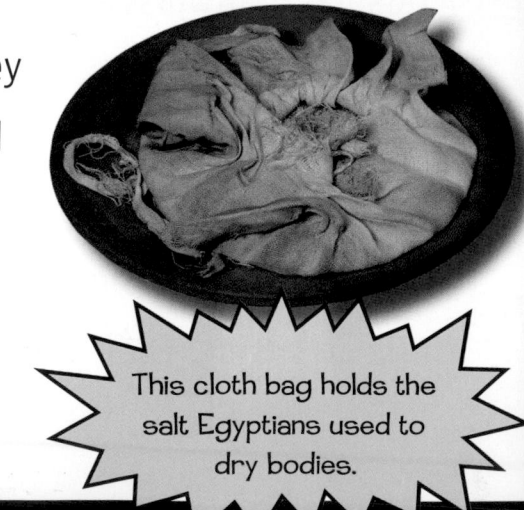

This cloth bag holds the salt Egyptians used to dry bodies.

Very cold air keeps bodies from decaying, too. Think of a freezer. If you left a strawberry on the counter, it would spoil. But if you kept it in the freezer, it would last longer. Many mummies have been found on the tops of mountains where the air is very cold and bacteria cannot grow to make a body decay.

Peat can turn bodies into mummies. But peat is not dry or icy. Peat is a very wet soil made of dead plants that have piled on top of each other. **Moss**, a type of plant, also grows with peat. This makes a **bog**. Bacteria can't grow in a peat bog. So bodies do not rot. Most "bog bodies" have been found in the peat bogs of Northern Europe.

A peat bog is a mixture of peat soil and moss. Bodies don't decay in peat bogs.

CHAPTER 4

The clothing, hair, and jewelry of a mummy tell us a lot about life long ago.

Archaeologists can learn a lot from a mummy. They can see what a person looked like. They can tell if it was a man or a woman and how old they were. They find clues about how the person died. They might even find food still in the mummy's stomach!

Archaeologists also learn a lot from the area around a mummy. They can tell if the person was rich or poor by the way the body was buried or by other remains nearby. Tools or weapons might tell scientists if the person was a hunter or farmer.

Remains are like puzzle pieces. The archaeologist

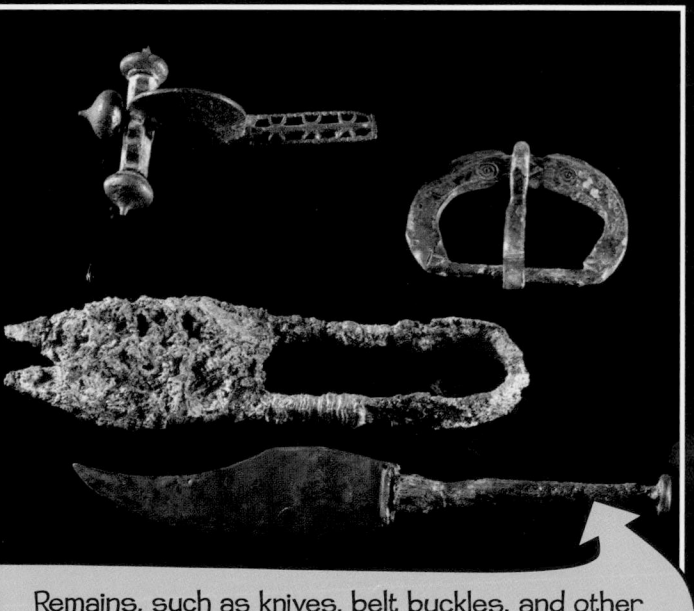

Remains, such as knives, belt buckles, and other tools, give scientists clues about how people lived.

Archaeologists study every bone they find to learn as much as they can about the past.

puts these bits of information together to make a picture of the past.
In 1991 a 5,300-year-old mummy called the "Iceman" was found in the
mountains in Italy. He still had his leather clothing, shoes, and fur hat.

He was frozen with his ax, dagger, bow, and arrows. His body and other remains told scientists a lot about how people dressed, worked, and lived during his time.

One of the most important things mummies tell scientists is how people of their time thought about death. The Egyptians thought a person needed his or her body for a new life after death. So they buried the mummy with food, money, clothes, and treasures, like they were packing for a long trip.

These gold sandals were buried with an Egyptian king for him to use in his life after death.

In Peru, the ruins of the city of Machu Picchu tell us a lot about the ways of a whole community.

The mummies in Peru were found in the mountains. The Incas **worshiped** the mountains. They buried children there as a gift to their gods. Water was important to people of Northern Europe. They put gifts, such as bowls or jewelry, in the bogs to honor their gods. They placed bodies there, too.

Mummies give archaeologists clues about how people lived hundreds or thousands of years ago. Mummies can't talk. But they can tell scientists a lot!

Look closely. That's what scientists do. They seek out remains to learn about people of the past.

Glossary

archaeology [ahr-kee-OL-uh-jee] the study of people from the past using the remains and objects they left behind

bacteria [bak-TEER-ee-uh] tiny living things that break down an item into soil

bog [BOG] spongy and wet ground

decay [di-KAY] to break down and turn into soil

dig [DIG] an area where scientists uncover remains of the past

moss [MAWS] a type of plant that grows like a mat on the ground

mummy [MUHM-ee] human remains that have not decayed over time

organs [OR-guhns] inside parts of the human body that each have a certain job to do

peat [PEET] a type of soil made from decayed plants

remains [ri-MAYNS] items left behind from life in the past

ruins [ROO-inz] the walls, stones, columns, or other remains of buildings left from cities of long ago

tombs [TOOMS] special places made to hold dead bodies

worshiped [WUR-shipt] honored and treated in a special way

Books to Discover

Deem, James M. *Bodies from the Ice: Melting Glaciers and the Recovery of the Past*. Boston, MA: Houghton Mifflin Company, 2008.

Halls, Kelly Milner. *Mysteries of the Mummy Kids*. Plain City, OH: Darby Creek Publishing, 2007.

Lauber, Patricia. *Who Came First? New Clues to Prehistoric Americans*. Washington, DC: National Geographic, 2003.

Malam, John. *Mummies*. Mankato, MN: Smart Apple Media, 2009.

Rubalcaba, Jill. *National Geographic Investigates: Ancient Egypt*. Washington, DC: 2006.

Websites to Explore

American Museum of Natural History www.amnh.org/

Dig: The Archaeology Magazine for Kids
www.digonsite.com/

NOVA: Ice Mummies of the Inca
www.pbs.org/wgbh/nova/peru/

Tutankhamun and the Golden Age of the Pharaohs Exhibit
www.kingtut.org/home

Index

About the Author

Dana Meachen Rau is the author of more than 250 books for children. She has written about many nonfiction topics from her home office in Burlington, Connecticut. Mrs. Rau once saw a King Tut exhibit and was stunned by all of his valuable treasures.

With thanks to the Reading Consultants:

Nanci R. Vargus, Ed.D., is an assistant professor of elementary education at the University of Indianapolis.

Beth Walker Gambro is an adjunct professor at the University of Saint Francis in Joliet, Illinois.